SandCastle

Long Vowels

Oō

Mary Elizabeth Salzmann

ABDO
Publishing Company

Published by SandCastle™, an imprint of ABDO Publishing Company, 4940 Viking Drive, Edina, Minnesota 55435.

Printed in the United States.

Cover and Interior Photo credits: Digital Stock, Eyewire Images, Photodisc, Rubberball Productions

Library of Congress Cataloging-in-Publication Data

Salzmann, Mary Elizabeth, 1968-
    Oo / Mary Elizabeth Salzmann.
      p. cm. -- (Long vowels)
    Includes index.
    ISBN 1-57765-416-1 (hardcover)
    ISBN 1-59197-048-2 (paperback)
      1. Readers (Primary) [1. English language--Phonetics.] I. Title.

PE1119 .S23424 2000
428.1--dc21

00-033206

The SandCastle concept, content, and reading method have been reviewed and approved by a national advisory board including literacy specialists, librarians, elementary school teachers, early childhood education professionals, and parents.

Let Us Know

After reading the book, SandCastle would like you to tell us your stories about reading. What is your favorite page? Was there something hard that you needed help with? Share the ups and downs of learning to read. We want to hear from you! To get posted on the Abdo Publishing Company Web site, send us email at:

sandcastle@abdopub.com

About SandCastle™

A professional team of educators, reading specialists, and content developers created the SandCastle™ series to support young readers as they develop reading skills and strategies and increase their general knowledge. The SandCastle™ series has four levels that correspond to early literacy development in young children. The levels are provided to help teachers and parents select the appropriate books for young readers.

Emerging Readers
(no flags)

Beginning Readers
(1 flag)

Transitional Readers
(2 flags)

Fluent Readers
(3 flags)

These levels are meant only as a guide. All levels are subject to change.

To see a complete list of SandCastle™ books and other nonfiction titles from ABDO Publishing Company, visit **www.abdopub.com** or contact us at:
4940 Viking Drive, Edina, Minnesota 55435 • 1-800-800-1312 • fax: 1-952-831-1632

I know many fun things
to do.

Don't you think so, too?

Olga uses a globe to locate Mexico.

The globe shows the whole world.

Olaf jumps over the fence on his way home from school.

Oleg practices playing the piano.

He has his piano lesson tomorrow.

Olivia and Enrico ride an old wooden horse.

Enrico holds the reins.

Olympia uses the phone to ask her friend Rose to come over.

We walk our dog by the ocean.

His name is Bo.

We end up rolling in the snow when we go sledding.

Opal uses a cone to cheer for her team.

What color is her cone?

(yellow)

Words I Can Read

Nouns

A noun is a person, place, or thing

color (KUHL-ur) p. 21
cone (KOHN) p. 21
dog (DOG) p. 17
fence (FENSS) p. 9
friend (FREND) p. 15
globe (GLOHB) p. 7
home (HOME) p. 9
horse (HORSS) p. 13

lesson (LESS-uhn) p. 11
name (NAYM) p. 17
ocean (OH-shuhn)
 p. 17
phone (FOHN) p. 15
piano (pee-AN-oh)
 p. 11
reins (RAYNZ) p. 13

school (SKOOL) p. 9
snow (SNOH) p. 19
team (TEEM) p. 21
things (THINGZ) p. 5
way (WAY) p. 9
world (WURLD) p. 7
yellow (YEL-oh) p. 21

Proper Nouns

A proper noun is the name
of a person, place, or thing

Bo (BOH) p. 17
Enrico (en-REE-coh)
 p. 13
Mexico (MEK-si-coh)
 p. 7

Olaf (OH-lahf) p. 9
Oleg (OH-leg) p. 11
Olga (OHL-guh) p. 7
Olivia (oh-LI-vee-uh)
 p. 13

Olympia (oh-LIM-pee-
 uh) p. 15
Opal (OH-puhl) p. 21
Rose (ROZE) p. 15

Pronouns

A pronoun is a word that replaces a noun

he (HEE) p. 11
I (EYE) p. 5

we (WEE) pp. 17, 19
what (WUHT) p. 21

you (YOO) p. 5

Verbs
A verb is an action or being word

ask (ASK) p. 15
cheer (CHIHR) p. 21
come (KUHM) p. 15
do (DOO) p. 5
don't (DOHNT) p. 5
end (END) p. 19
go (GOH) p. 19
has (HAZ) p. 11
holds (HOHLDZ) p. 13

is (IZ) pp. 17, 21
jumps (JUHMPSS) p. 9
know (NOH) p. 5
locate (LOH-kate) p. 7
playing (PLAY-ing) p. 11
practices (PRAK-tiss-ez) p. 11
ride (RIDE) p. 13

rolling (ROHL-ing) p. 19
shows (SHOHZ) p. 7
sledding (SLED-ing) p. 19
think (THINGK) p. 5
uses (YOOZ-ez) pp. 7, 15, 21
walk (WAWK) p. 17

Adjectives
An adjective describes something

fun (FUHN) p. 5
her (HUR) pp. 15, 21
his (HIZ) pp. 9, 11, 17
many (MEN-ee) p. 5

old (OHLD) p. 13
our (AR) p. 17
piano (pee-AN-oh) p. 11

whole (HOLE) p. 7
wooden (WUD-en) p. 13

Adverbs
An adverb tells how, when, or where something happens

over (OH-vur) p. 15
so (SOH) p. 5

tomorrow (tuh-MOR-oh) p. 11

too (TOO) p. 5
up (UHP) p. 19

Glossary

globe – a round model of the world.

ocean – the huge bodies of salt water that cover most of the world.

reins – straps that control or guide a horse.

world – the planet Earth.

More Oō Words

also	hello	open
both	joke	pony
close	koala	robot
drove	low	social
flow	most	told
ghost	note	zero